In Memory of

_____

(full name)

Presented to _____

By _____

Date _____

When
Loved Ones
Are
Called Home

Herbert Wernecke

Baker Book House
Grand Rapids, Michigan

Standard Book
Number: 8010-9504-2

Library of Congress
Catalog Card Number: 69-15665

Copyright 1950
by Herbert H. Wernecke

Twentieth Printing, May, 1970

Printed in the United States of America
by Malloy Lithographing, Inc.,
Ann Arbor, Michigan

Dedicated to the
Blessed Memory and Continuing
Influence of
IDA A. WERNECKE (1899-1947)
Devoted and Loyal Companion
for Over a Quarter of a Century

When God sends forth a spotless soul
To learn the ways of earth,
A MOTHER'S LOVE is waiting here;
We call this wonder BIRTH.

When God calls home a tired soul,
And stills a fitful breath,
LOVE DIVINE is waiting there,
This, too, is BIRTH, not death.

Foreword

To the Christian, death should not be a morbid subject. And yet we need to confess that we have too often repressed and put out of mind all serious consideration and discussion of death. Some one has suggested that we are now repressing discussion of death the way we used to do about sex. Yet death is a fact of our lives, and the lives of those we love. And there is a Christian attitude toward death and grief and bereavement. Anything which can help us to see this, to stimulate us to see the Christian attitude is of great importance. We need to consider death *before* it occurs to those we love.

When death has occurred to a friend or family member, we naturally feel lost for a time, however deep our faith. There is no substitute for the pain of acute grief. But when that has begun to change from a sharp pain to a dull emptiness, then we seek eagerly and properly for new light on the Christian meaning of death and grief.

I believe Dr. Wernecke's book will prove useful both to those who have experienced bereavement, and to others who want light on the Christian attitude even before a personal grief experience. He writes out of personal experience and a deep Christian faith.

— SEWARD HILTNER

All that tread
The globe are but a handful to the tribes
That slumber in its bosom.

WILLIAM CULLEN BRYANT, *Thanatopsis*

The words in the title of this booklet say much in a few words. The aim is to help loved ones to understand more clearly something of what is involved for those who leave us and those who are left behind that we may realize more fully the meaning of Paul's words, "But I would not have you to be ignorant, brethren, concerning them which are asleep, that ye sorrow not, even as others which have no hope" (I Thes. 4:13); and Jesus' words, "Let not your heart be troubled, neither let it be afraid" (John 14:27).

The Christian views the departure of loved ones in the faith as a home-going. They are "at home with the Lord" (II Cor. 5:8). This is our faith and blessed is he who enjoys a fair measure of it — for there is no other support that can be compared with it when the "silver cord is broken." This faith is "our sure and steadfast hope" (Heb. 6:19) that enables us not merely to bear the pain of separation but to become so reconciled to suddenly interrupted plans and new adjustments that confront us that we can bow humbly and say, "The Lord hath given, the Lord hath taken away, blessed be the name of the Lord," (Job 1:21).

Death As Home-Going

When all is done, say not my day is o'er
And that through night I seek a dimmer shore;
Say rather that my morn has just begun.

I greet the dawn and not a setting sun,
When all is done.

While they who are asleep in Jesus are thus safe
from suffering, from sorrow, and from sin, we also
are drawn nearer to heaven as we watch them
entering. The door stands ajar a moment and we
catch glimpses of what is within. The death of
friends opens our eyes to many truths which we
have but dimly discerned before, and gives a pre-
ciousness to what has been only an intellectual
belief.

— JOHN O. MEANS

The incisive criticisms of the first manuscript by The
Rev. Dr. Robert M. Trenery, Chaplain of City Hospital,
St. Louis, Missouri and by the Rev. R. Huenemann,
Pastor of Zion Church, Lodi, California, are especially
appreciated. They represent two significant areas, the
Hospital and the Christian congregation, where a dis-
tinct need is keenly felt for the all-sufficient comfort
our Christian faith offers.

— HERBERT H. WERNECKE

Contents

The lily of the valley,
a flower long symbolic of Christ
(Song of Solomon 2:1), points to the
beauty and purity found in Christ.
This lily, very much at home in
the deep valley, suggests the
nearness of Christ in the valley of death.

I

GOD COMFORTS

US AND HEALS THE

WOUND OF SEPARATION

Your loved one has departed from your side. It is only natural that you should feel an aching void, that grief should weigh you down, and that your tears should flow. This is well. Do not unduly suppress your emotions. Jesus too, wept at Lazarus' tomb. Do not put on a mask of "all's well" when your heart is breaking. Physical expression of your emotions is the God-ordained safety valve to protect you from physical, mental, and spiritual destruction in this hour of grief.

On the other hand, do not allow yourself to become the slave of your emotions. To mourn as one who has no hope is unbecoming to your position as a Christian

17

witness. And to prolong your grief through careful nursing of it is a sin against God, and an injustice to yourself and to those with whom you associate. God has left you behind because he has some work for you to do before he also takes you home. He expects you to adjust yourself to this environment from which your loved one is so painfully absent. It may seem well nigh impossible, but remember

> His grace is sufficient, whate'er may befall,
>> Perhaps, even now, you may hear His sweet call;
> "Come, cast upon Me all thy conflicts and care;
>> I'll carry thy burdens, thy sorrows I'll share;
> In faithfulness I all thy comfort shall be,
>> I'll give consolation, O, come unto Me."
>
> — SELECTED

It is no doubt helpful to analyze in as detailed a manner as possible the various elements that go to make up our grief, whether in this crisis with which we are dealing here or in others. The really satisfying comfort must be sought, however, elsewhere than in mere mental readjustments or proper psychological approaches. Before we turn to these more helpful sources of comfort, a word ought to be said about

The Healing Balm of Time

Time in itself is a great healer — another one of God's gracious provisions for us. The further you are removed from an experience in time, other things being equal, the less it affects you for weal or woe.

We must recognize that the healing process is a slow one — that there will be empty days, poignant grief, seemingly unbearable loneliness and pain, even resistance to consolation and disinterestedness in life. But he who promised "as thy days so shall thy strength be," in His gracious Providence causes these wounds to gradually grow less painful, and give way to the healing sunlight of love, friendship and the challenging duties of life itself.

> Time like an ever-rolling stream
> Bears all our grief away.

The Ministry of Friends

Then there is the gracious ministry of friends. "Where one member suffers, all members suffer with it" (I Cor. 12:26).

"Rejoice with them that rejoice; weep with them that weep" (Rom. 12:15).

> We share our mutual woes,
> Our mutual burdens bear,
> And often for each other flows
> The sympathizing tear.

Just the presence of friends without a word spoken can be precious. But most of all do we find healing with those who have suffered a sorrow like our own. Deepest understanding comes out of like experience.

> Oh, ray of light, *my friend!*
> When sorrow's gloom made life so drear,
> Then comfort sweet thy words did lend,
> As if Christ spake, "Be of good cheer!"

Oh, rock of strength, *my friend!*
  When shifting sands beneath my feet
And changing scenes my steps attend,
  Thy truth and constancy are sweet.

I clasp thy hand, *my friend!*
  Thank God that thou art here;
I am not worthy He should send
  To me a gift so dear.

— AUTHOR UNKNOWN

God's Comforting Promises

Our chief comfort is Jesus Himself.

> What a friend we have in Jesus,
> All our sins and *griefs* to bear.

Jesus' words are understood by the grief-stricken soul with new clarity and deeper meaning.

"Let not your heart be troubled: ye believe in God, believe also in me. In my Father's house are many mansions: if it were not so, I would have told you. I go to prepare a place for you" (John 14:1, 2).

"I will not leave you comfortless: I will come to you" (John 14:18).

"Come unto me, all ye that labour and are heavy laden, and I will give you rest" (Matt. 11:28).

"Verily, verily, I say unto you, He that heareth my word, and believeth on him that sent me, hath everlasting life, and shall not come into condemnation; but is passed from death unto life" (John 5:24).

The messages of prophets, evangelists and apostles supplement and illuminate those of Jesus.

> I opened the old, old Bible,
> And looked at a page of Psalms
> Till the wintry sea of my troubles
> Was soothed as by summer calms;
> For the words that have helped so many,
> And the ages have made more dear,
> Seemed new in their power to comfort,
> As they brought me their word of cheer.
>
> — AUTHOR UNKNOWN

"The Lord is my shepherd; I shall not want" (Ps. 23). No other Old Testament words have brought more comfort to souls in distress than this Shepherd Psalm. Millions have had their faith strengthened through Paul's great resurrection chapter, First Corinthians 15. Peter, the Apostle of Hope, has brought encouragement to countless others. John, the Apostle of Love, reveals Him who is the light and life of men.

II

DEATH,

A REVERENCE-INSPIRING

EXPERIENCE

To see our loved ones pass on, to see them, so far as this world goes, entering the eternal silence, breathe their last breath is a reverence-inspiring experience. Then as in no other way and at no other time, the words of the Psalmist come home to us, "Thou sayest, Return ye children of men" (90:3). We are in the presence of the Lord of life. Physicians and surgeons, nurses and loved ones — all have done their utmost to prolong life but in God's mysterious yet gracious Providence, the end has come.

The Finality of It

The life of that loved one is now beyond recall. We can think back and remember all that he has meant to us, how life was enriched through him; but nothing that we can say or do, no matter what we are willing to offer of labor or sacrifice, can bring him back.

Nor would we ultimately want to, if we truly believe that our life is in God's hands and "He doeth all things well." Hardly would any of us feel capable of assuming the responsibility of saying when any person's life should end.

Accepting the Fact of Death

We suffer when loved ones pass on, partly because we are unprepared for this separation. While we recognize that sooner or later death will come to all of us, when it does come into our circle, we are shocked, often confused and upset.

To be mature, grown-up to the point of facing the realities of life, includes the recognition that death can come to us or our loved ones any moment and requires an adjustment to this fact accordingly.

Baron Rothschild left one corner of the foundation of his house unfinished that he might constantly be reminded "For here have we no continuing city, but we seek one to come" (Heb. 3:14).

Nothing is more certain than the fact of death; nothing is more uncertain than the time of death.

Some may agree with Bacon that it is as natural to die as to be born, but we find more comfort in the more profound word of Paul, "For the wages of sin is death; but the gift of God is eternal life through Jesus

Christ our Lord" (Rom. 6:23). When a child is born into the world, we cannot predict whether he will be rich or poor, what occupation he will follow or where he will live; but we can declare positively that one day he will die.

Seeing Death as Jesus Viewed It

Death is not extinction. It is not the end of life. True, it is the end of this state of existence. The separation of the soul from the body does not mean the destruction of the soul, but rather a sleep and an awakening in a better land. We must always remember that we bury only the body of our loved one; the soul has gone to be with its Lord.

One day in his eightieth year John Quincy Adams was tottering down a Boston street. He was accosted by a friend who said, "And how is John Quincy Adams today?"

The former president of the United States replied graciously, "Thank you, John Quincy Adams is well, sir, quite well, I thank you. But the house in which he lives at present is becoming dilapidated. It is tottering upon its foundations. Time and the seasons have nearly destroyed it. Its roof is pretty well worn out, its walls are much shattered, and it trembles with every wind. The old tenement is becoming almost uninhabitable, and I think John Quincy Adams will have to move out of it soon; but he himself is quite well, sir, quite well." And with this the venerable statesman, leaning heavily upon his cane, moved slowly down the street.

John Quincy Adams had the same assurance which we all have. He knew that "if the earthly house of our tabernacle be dissolved, we have a building from God, a house not made with hands, eternal, in the heavens" (II Cor. 5:1).

If we fear or question the future, we have not come to a true realization of Jesus' counsel, "Let not your heart be troubled I go to prepare a place for you . . . that where I am, there ye may be also."

Job's question, "If a man die, shall he live again?" the question of every grief-stricken heart, is answered by the words of Jesus, "Because I live, ye shall live also."

A few days before his death, F. B. Meyer wrote a very dear friend these words: "I have just heard, to my surprise, that I have only a few more days to live. It may be that, before this reaches you, I shall have entered the Palace. Don't trouble to write. We shall meet in the morning."

The experience that the world calls death is, in the New Testament, referred to frequently as a sleep. Of Jairus' daughter Jesus said, "She is not dead, but sleepeth." "Our friend Lazarus sleepeth."

> "David, after he had served his own generation by the will of God, fell on sleep"; Stephen "fell asleep"; "Them also which sleep in Jesus"; these are only a few of the many examples of the use of the word. The expression is sweetly significant.
>
> Sleep is transitory. It implies a reawakening. The Bible calls bodily death a "sleep" for the reason that the death state is not eternal, but only temporary, from which there is presently to come a rising up again. That is not sleep which has no awakening to follow. It is said that at three o'clock one morning, A. T. Pierson,

received a telegram, asking him to preach the sermon at the funeral of A. J. Gordon. Unable to sleep, he spent the rest of the night searching His Greek Testament for what it said about death. He made an important discovery. He confessed before the great throng gathered for the occasion, his surprise to find that after the resurrection, the apostles never used the word *death* to express the close of a Christian's earthly life; but referred to the passing of a Christian as "at home with the Lord," "to depart and be with Christ," "to sleep in Jesus," "fallen asleep," "loosing the mooring," "forever with the Lord," and in similar terms.

Think of a small boy at the end of a happy day. He seldom regards sleep as a friend. Rather would he keep on playing with his toys. But after a while, most reluctantly, he lies down to sleep in his mother's arms. Then the weary body begins to relax. The touch of fever departs from his brow. In the early morning, he awakens in newness of life, and rejoices in powers equal to the new day's tasks.

> God is! Christ loves! Christ lives!
> And by His own Returning gives
>   Sure proofs of Immortality,
>   The first fruits He: and we
>   The harvest of His victory.
> The life beyond shall this life far transcend,
> And death is the beginning not the end.

Necessary Readjustments

A vacant chair in the family circle and in the circle of friends compels painful readjustments. The more devoted the relationship has been, the greater the interdependence, the more painful is the change.

There are the physical readjustments of economic

factors which alone may seem like a crushing burden. Even more painful will be the social adjustments of dependent children, left without father or without mother, the lonesomeness and at times helplessness of the widow or the widower, and all the more of those left without any family relationships. We cannot, without pain, be separated for even a few weeks from those we deeply love. How much greater the sadness and loneliness when the separation includes the remainder of our mortal life!

Still, these broken relationships can be adjusted and in some way provided for, but the new relationship of spirit to spirit or soul to soul is felt still more keenly. For a time there will be acute pain but as indicated in Chapter I, God gradually heals the wound and we become not only reconciled to the physical absence of our loved one, but come to see God's gracious Hand in it all.

Just Away

I cannot say and I will not say
That he is dead — "he is just away."
With a cheery smile and a wave of the hand
He has wandered into an unknown land,
And left us dreaming how very fair
It needs must be since he lingers there.
And you — O you, who the wildest yearn
For the old-time step and glad return,
Think of him as faring on, as dear
In the love of *There* as the love of *Here*.
Think of him still as the same, I say;
He is not dead — he is just away

— James Witcomb Riley

Many a sensitive soul finds that after the first shock of separation has passed, the loved one is in spirit closer than ever before. Death breaks down the barriers of time and space. So Stanton, in his funeral eulogy of Abraham Lincoln, could declare, "Now he belongs to the ages."

LOVE KEEPS ITS OWN ETERNALLY

I cannot think of them as dead
    Who walk with me no more;
Along the path of life I tread
    They have but gone before.

The Father's house is mansioned fair
    Beyond my vision dim;
All souls are His, and here or there
    Are living unto Him.

And still their silent ministry
    Within my heart hath place,
As when on earth they walked with me
    And met me face to face.

Their lives are made forever mine;
    What they to me have been,
Hath left henceforth its seal and sign
    Engraven deep within.

Mine are they by an ownership
    Nor time nor death can free;
For God hath giv'n to Love to keep
    Its own eternally.

— FREDERICK HOSMER

The destination of my God
Is not within the grave's cold walls;
But where the bells of Heaven toll,
I'll soar whene'er my Savior calls!

Yea, far beyond the starry sky
There is a land bereft of care;
When to its glories I draw nigh
I'll see my Savior standing there!

With smiling face he'll bid me come,
And lead me to a mansion fair:
O day of days! When I reach home —
What joy! What bliss beyond compare!

The destination of my Soul,
Is not beneath the cold, gray sod;
But when the bells of Heaven toll,
I'll soar to meet my Living God!

We had nothing to do with our coming into this world, yet when we arrived, there was a place all prepared for us by the loving care and thought of our parents and friends. Can we not expect the same when we depart from this life?

This conviction, based on the limitless resources of our Christian faith, will enable us to accept and face bravely whatever detailed adjustments must be made and whatever detailed problems will arise.

It Is Not Death To Die

It is not death to die,
To leave this weary road,
And midst the brotherhood on high
To be at home with God.

It is not death to close
The eye long dimmed by tears,
And wake, in glorious repose
To spend eternal years.

It is not death to bear
The wrench that sets us free
From dungeon chain, to breathe
The air of boundless liberty.

Jesus, Thou Prince of life!
Thy chosen cannot die;
Like Thee, they conquer in the strife,
To reign with Thee on high.

III

DEATH,

THE GATEWAY

INTO LIFE EVERLASTING

May not the end of the journey be more joyous than the beginning? Usually we rejoice at the birth of a child but mourn when loved ones pass on. If we considered more thoughtfully what is involved in each event, possibly our reaction would be quite different.

First of all, we may say, there is more mystery surrounding birth than death. How little do we really know about the origin of life beyond the words of Genesis, "In the beginning God created the heavens and the earth" (1:1), and more specifically, "God created man in his own image, in the image of God created He him" (1:27). Similarly with its implications, John's words assert that God is the ultimate source of our life: "Jesus . . . knowing that he was come from God, and went to God" (John 13:3). Beyond this simple fact, our origin is not described. The Bible deals in much greater detail with the present and the future than with the past.

Our interest just now concerns the future. Even omitting prophecies whose specific meanings are frequently disputed, we have a considerable portion of Jesus' own words dealing directly with things to come. His post-resurrection appearances are a glimpse into the future. Every one of the New Testament books, directly or by implication, sheds light upon the things that are to come to pass, beyond this age in which we are living.

On the basis of what we know this world to be and what we believe the future holds in store for God's children, there is good reason for saying that the end of our journey here should be more joyous than its beginning.

The uncertainties, the anxieties, the suffering, the pain, the misunderstandings — the fruits of sin in one form or another — are unavoidable here. At its best, life is a struggle against evil forces, within and without, that cause many a devoted servant of God to sob, "O Lord, how long?" That life is so imperfect and incomplete, so full of confusion and even despair is one of the tragedies of our present existence. "The good that I would, I do not; the evil that I would not, that I do" (Rom. 7:19).

On the other hand, the teaching of Jesus and his apostles and the glorious imagery of Revelation disclose to us that "Now we see in a glass darkly but then face to face; now I know in part, but then shall I know even as also I am known" (I Cor. 13:12).

To the extent that we by faith have accepted God's forgiveness and pardon in Jesus Christ, so that the course of sin is removed, death becomes a *home-going*.

John Oxenham has well expressed this Christian view of death in the following lines:

Shapeless and grim,
A Shadow dim,
O'erhung my ways
And darkened all my days.
And all who saw,
With bated breath,
Said, "It is Death!"

And I, in weakness,
Slipping toward the night,
In sore affright
Looked up. And lo! —
No Specter grim,
But just a dim,
Sweet face,
A sweet, high mother-face
A face like Christ's own mother's face

Alight with tenderness
And grace.
"Thou art not Death," I cried —
For Life's supremest fantasy
Had never thus envisaged Death to me —
"Thou art not Death, the End!"

In accents winning
Came the answer: "Friend,
There is no Death!
I am the Beginning,
Not the End!"

Truly, we may rejoice when God unfolds a new life, as infants come to bless our homes and gradually take the place God has planned for them here, but to those of experience and deeper insight it cannot be unmingled joy. Likewise are our hearts saddened when loved ones are called from our side or out of our circle; but it need not be an experience of unmingled sadness for, though death leaves us lonely for the tender physical presence that we miss, our hearts may be glad for the happiness of those who have passed through death to life. "For me to live is Christ, to die is gain" (Phil. 1:21). For such the words apply, *"For* Christ here, *with* Christ yonder."

More Love and Beauty There

When loved ones cross the sunset sea
God never meant that there should be
Lonely hours of sorrow for
Those who are left upon the shore.

For if He filled this world of ours
With love and stars and fragrant flowers
How can we doubt His tender care
Will give more love and beauty there?

A Prayer

O death, thou angel of God, thou dost seem to rob us of our Treasures; but thou dost really make them ours forever in the dew of an immortal youth, transfiguring them with a light that can never fade from their faces or our lives; blotting out only what we are glad to forget, preserving what we loved in imperishable beauty.

— F. B. Meyer

No Disappointment In Heaven

There's no disappointment in Heaven
   No weariness, sorrow or pain
No hearts that are bleeding and broken
   No song with a minor refrain:
The clouds of our earthly horizon
   Will never appear in the sky,
For all will be sunshine and gladness
   With never a sob or a sigh.

There'll never be crepe on the door-knob
   No funeral train in the sky,
No grave on the hillside of glory
   For there men shall nevermore die.
The old will be young there forever
   Transformed in a moment of time;
Immortal will stand in His likeness
   The stars and the sun to outshine.

I'm bound for the beautiful city
   My Lord has prepared for his own,
Where all the redeemed of all ages,
   Sing glory because they are home.
Sometimes I grow homesick for heaven
   And the glories I there shall behold.
What a joy that will be when my Savior I see
   In that beautiful city of gold.

And God shall wipe away all tears from their eyes (Rev. 21:4).

A City without tears — God wipes away all tears up yonder. This is a time of weeping, but by and by there will be a time when God shall call us where there will be no tears. A City without pain, a City without sorrow, without sickness, without death . . . Think of a place where temptation cannot come. Think of a place where we shall be free from sin . . . and where the righteous shall reign forever. Think of a City that is not built with hands, where the buildings do not grow old with time; a City whose inhabitants are numbered by no census, except the Book of Life . . . Think of a City . . . where no hearses with their nodding plumes creep slowly with their sad burdens to the cemetery; a City without griefs or graves, without sins or sorrows, without marriages or mournings, without births or burials; a City which glories in having Jesus for its King, angels for its guards, and whose citizens are saints.

— DWIGHT L. MOODY

THE FAITH THAT COMFORTS

I go to life and not to death
From darkness to life's native sky;
I go from sickness and from pain
To health and immortality.
Let our farewell, then, be tearless,
Since I bid farewell to tears;
Write this day of my departure
Festive in your coming years.

— HORATIUS BONAR

Physical death is the separation of the soul from the body. While it seems to end all, basically nothing has been lost. Since Jesus has robbed death of its sting and the grave of its victory, death for the believer is not the dreaded door into oblivion. Rather has it been transformed into the gate of life. "For the believer, death was destroyed *de jure* at the cross (II Tim. 1: 10) and will be abolished *de facto* in glory" (I Cor. 15:26).

When the great Puritan, Owen, lay on his deathbed, his secretary wrote (in his name) to a friend, "I am still in the land of the living." "Stop," said Owen, "change that and say, 'I am yet in the land of the dying, but I hope soon to be in the land of the living.'"

"Therefore we are always confident, knowing that, whilst we are at home in the body we are absent from the Lord" (II Cor. 5:8).

The Living and the Dead

The living are the only dead;
  The dead live — nevermore to die;
And often when we mourn them fled,
  They never were so nigh.

O, why should memory veil'd with gloom,
  And like a sorrowing mourner draped,
Sit weeping o'er an empty tomb
  Whose captives have escaped!

'Tis but a mound — and will be mossed
  Whene'er the Summer grass appears;

39

The loved, though wept, are never lost;
   We only lose our tears.

The joys we lose are but forecast
   And we shall find them all once more;
We look behind us for the past,
   But lo! 'Tis all before!

And though they lie beneath the waves,
   Or sleep within the churchyard dim —
Ah! Through how many different graves
   God's children go to Him.

ON THE DEATH OF A BELIEVER

In vain our fancy strives to paint
   The moment after death,
The glories that surround the saints,
   When yielding up their breath.

One gentle sigh their fetters breaks;
   We scarce can say, "They're gone!"
Before the willing spirit takes
   Her mansion near the throne.

Faith strives, but all its efforts fail,
   To trace her in her flight!
No eye can pierce within the veil
   Which hides that world of light.

Thus much (and this is all) we know,
   They are completely bless'd;
Have done with sin, and care, and woe,
   And with their Saviour rest.

On harps of gold they praise his name,
  His face they always view;
Then let us foll'wers be of them,
  That we may praise him too.

Their faith and patience, love and zeal,
  Should make their mem'ry dear;
And, Lord, do thou the pray'rs fulfill
  They offer'd for us here.

While they have gain'd, we losers are,
  We miss them day by day;
But thou canst ev'ry breach repair,
  And wipe our tears away.

We pray, as in Elisha's case,
  When great Elijah went
May double portions of thy grace,
  To us who stay, be sent.

— I. NEWTON, *d.* 1807,
The Olney Hymnal

IV

QUESTIONS

THAT PUZZLE AND DISTRESS

How Can God Do This to Me?

This is a legitimate question when loved ones are called from our side, because the answer will help us definitely to find our God-appointed place in His total plan. Possibly it can be answered indirectly by asking, "Why should this *not* happen to *me?* Is there any reason why I should escape the sorrow and heartaches of others?"

"An Eastern legend tells of a woman who lost her only child. In her grief she went to a prophet and begged him to restore the child to her. The old man looked long and understandingly at her, and then tenderly counseled, 'Go and bring me a handful of rice from some home where sorrow has not entered and I shall grant your wish."

The little Oriental mother began her search. Here and there she went; but always the reply to her question was the same. In every dwelling there was an empty chair at the table, a vacant seat before the hearth.

Slowly the sorrow of others touched her sorrowing heart. Soon her sympathy went out to them in their grief. Gradually the waves of her own despair subsided. She found comfort in the universal presence of sorrow.

Death is an unavoidable part of our experience on this planet. When it comes, no bird stops its singing, all life continues to move along oblivious to our personal sorrow. At first this seems very cruel. But on second thought it reveals the naturalness of the experience. Every moment marks the passing of someone into the Great Beyond, a loved-one of some family, friend or neighbor.

Why? Why? I Just Can't Understand It!

On the one hand, who are we to question God's wisdom and ways? Should we not rather come to the conclusion of Job: The universe is in Thy hands, O God, I realize thy majesty and power. To Job's thoughts we can add the words of Paul in Romans 8: 28: "And we know that all things work together for good to them that love God, to them who are the called according to his purpose." Also II Corinthians 4:17, 18: "For our light affliction, which is but for a moment, worketh for us a far more exceeding and eternal weight of glory; While we look not at the things which are seen, but at the things which are not seen; for the things which are seen are temporal; but the things which are not seen are eternal."

Likewise do Jesus' words to Peter apply here: "What I do thou knowest not now; but thou shalt know hereafter" (John 13:7).

Sometime We'll Understand

Not now, but in the coming years,
    It may be in the Better Land,
We'll read the meaning of our tears,
    And there, sometime, we'll understand.

We'll catch the broken threads again,
    And finish what we here began;
Heav'n will the mysteries explain,
    And then, ah, then, we'll understand.

We'll know why clouds instead of sun
    Were over many a cherished plan;
Why song has ceased, when scarce begun;
    'Tis there, sometime, we'll understand.

God knows the way, He holds the key,
    He guides us with unerring hand;
Sometimes with tearless eyes we'll see;
    Yes, there, up there, we'll understand.

Then trust in God through all thy days;
    Fear not, for he doth hold thy hand;

Though dark the way, still sing and praise;
Sometime, sometime, we'll understand.
— MAXWELL N. CORNELIUS

We are so constituted that we feel impelled to reason things out as far as we can, and that is well.
While it is our sacred duty to preserve life, to do all
that is within our power to sustain it, there are circum-
stances beyond our control (accidents, calamities, er-
rors of judgment on the part of ourselves or others)
which lead to the cessation of life as we know it here.

We accept the unchangeable as in some sense the
will of God, events that have occurred by his permis-
sive decree. Blessed is he who can bow in humble
submission at such a time and say, "Not my will but
thine, O Father, be done." In his Fatherly Providence
we can confidently place our trust.

If Only I Had . . .

"The cancer of regret" we may call this self-accusa-
tion, this blaming of one's self for things that are unchangeable and might just as likely as not have been
made worse than better if ours had been the ability to
change them.

Naturally there is a place for sincere repentance for
neglect and wrong-doing, if these are involved. But
there is also the assurance of forgiveness whenever there
is genuine Christian repentance.

Most frequently, however this question reflects not a
feeling of actual guilt but a measure of desperation
as at times we speculate how the sorrowful outcome

might perhaps have been avoided: "If I had taken the first illness more seriously," "If we had called in the doctor earlier," "If we had only moved south instead of north."

> So spoke Martha also in John 11, "*If* Thou hadst been here!" But he had been there all the time. He had been with them in deepest sympathy, in kindly thought, in gracious intention, in tender and yet ample plan. What they viewed as a lamentable mischance was a vital part of a larger scheme, begotten and inspired by unfailing love. There was no need for regret; everything was just exactly right.
>
> And so it is with most of the *if's*, the remorseful *if's* that ravage and devastate our peace. They destroy filial trust; they destroy spiritual peace; they destroy the wide sweeping light of Christian hope."
>
> — J. H. JOWETT

And supposing we have made mistakes, is it not the essence of the gospel of His grace that He can repair the things that are broken, reset the joints of the bruised reed, restore the broken heart? Let us, then, rather be grateful for the blessings God has permitted us to enjoy, and accept the painful experiences of life as also a part of his total Providence.

Why Must We Go When We Are So Anxious To Remain Here?

There are within us two conflicting tendencies — the love of life here and the desire to be at home with Christ, both divinely implanted.

To the first tendency we owe the desire, even the

47

obligation, to sustain and nurture human life to the utmost. Upon it rests the realization that human life is sacred and that its termination here is in God's hands. Related to this are the various ties that bind us to loved ones and to our present environment.

Yet, most of us lack a proper perspective and regard this life as too important as compared with the realm beyond. While it is true that our immediate duty and obligations are to this world now, "we have here no continuing city, but we seek one to come" (Heb. 13: 14). "Our citizenship is in heaven; from whence also we look for the Saviour, the Lord Jesus Christ: Who shall change our vile body, that it may be fashioned like unto his glorious body, according to the working whereby he is able even to subdue all things unto himself" (Phil. 3:20, 21).

> Light of eternity, Light divine
> Into this darkness shine,
> That the small may appear small
> And the great greatest of all
> Light of eternity, shine!

That is the sane, the proper approach to life as we know it in its totality. Such perspective will make us content to sojourn here and at the same time be not only willing but glad to follow the Master's call whenever it comes to us.

Why Does God Permit Suffering?

The problem of the suffering of the innocent is older than Job. When we or society disobey God's law of health, we can expect sickness and the suffering that goes with it. Incurable diseases, unavoidable accidents, premature deaths of all kinds serve to remind us that life is a gift of God which we hold as a sacred trust until he chooses to call us home.

When we find no cause and hence see no reason for our suffering, we can still let the experience serve to glorify God. The man born blind did not suffer blindness because he had sinned nor because of his parents' sin, but "that the works of God should be made manifest in him" (John 8:3). There is no convincing, satisfying answer to the question of innocent suffering. It remains a mystery. But suffering has been and can be the occasion for coming into deeper fellowship with God and a more sympathetic understanding of mankind. The sickness, the sorrow, the suffering which has entered our lives can equip us for helping and strengthening others, that "We may be able to comfort them which are in any trouble, by the comfort wherewith we ourselves are comforted of God" (II Cor. 1:4).

Repeatedly we have been reminded that far more important than *what* we suffer is *how* we suffer: how we use that experience, how it affects us, what we do as a result of it. Martin Luther, while fighting on behalf of freedom of conscience, was hampered by gravel, headache and earache. John Calvin suffered such violent migraine attacks and gout that he could scarcely crawl from bed to writing table. Handicapped, defective, deformed bodies have challenged valiant souls, in the words of Paul Scherer, "to weave life's defeats into

49

battleflags and made them to wave in the winds of misfortune."

LORD, TAKE AWAY PAIN

The cry of man's anguish went up unto God,
   "Lord, take away pain!
The shadow that darkens the world Thou hast made;
   The close-coiling chain
That strangles the heart; the burden that weighs on the
     wings
     that would soar —
Lord, take away from the world Thou hast made.
   That it love Thee the more!" —

Then answered the Lord to the cry of His world;
   "Shall I take away pain,
And with it the power of the soul to endure,
   Made strong by the strain?
Shall I take away pity, that knits heart to heart,
   And sacrifice high?
Will ye lose all your heroes that lift from the fire
White brows to the sky?
Shall I take away love, that redeems with a price,
   And smiles at its loss?
Can ye spare from your lives that would climb unto mine
   The Christ on His Cross?"
     — FOUND ON THE WALL OF A DENVER HOSPITAL

LESSONS IN GRACE

*"Yea, I have loved Thee with an
everlasting love"* (Jer. 31:3).

I have been through the valley of weeping,
   The valley of sorrow and pain;
But the "God of all comfort" was with me,
   At hand to uphold and sustain.

As the earth needs the clouds and the sunshine,
  Our souls need both sorrow and joy;
So He places us oft in the furnace,
  The dross from the gold to destroy.

When He leads through some valley of trouble
  His omnipotent hand we can trace;
For the trials and sorrows He sends us
  Are parts of His lessons in grace.

Well He knows that affliction is needed;
  He has a wise purpose in view;
And in the dark valley He whispers:
  "Hereafter, thou'lt know what to do."

As we travel through life's shadowed valley,
  Fresh springs of His love ever rise;
And we learn that our sorrows and losses
  Are blessings just sent in disguise.

So we'll follow wherever He leadeth,
  Let the path be dreary or bright;
For we've proved that God can give comfort;
  Our God can give songs in the night.

— From *Streams in the Desert*

What Gain Does Death Bring?

Death for the Christian is not an "irreparable loss," a "fearful thing"; but rather do we join with Paul, saying, "To die is gain" — a deliverance, a new beginning, an entrance into a larger sphere of life experience, fellowship and service. Death is not a state of unconscious sleep and insensibility. It is a state of recognition and remembrance. While we are unable to grasp with any degree of fulness the details, there are thrilling intimations in the New Testament of what awaits the believer.

Paul declares that the believer will be immediately with Christ. He exchanges time for eternity. Time is a probationary period filled with toils and trials, tears and disappointments. Eternity is a settled state with steady progress in life and knowledge. He exchanges comparative darkness for clear light. "Now we see through a glass darkly; but then face to face." He exchanges present limited knowledge for a knowledge commensurate with his new state. "Now I know in part; but then shall I know even as also I am known" (I Cor. 13:12).

The old sinful nature that led so often to discouragement and defeat has been definitely broken. The redeemed by the grace of God can *put it off* (Eph. 4:22); *keep it under* (I Cor. 9:27); *reckon it to be dead* (Rom. 6:11); *make no provision for it* (Rom. 13:14); they can now walk completely after the Spirit and not fulfill the lusts of the flesh.

Death is gain because it brings the believer into the most congenial fellowship and environment. "And there shall in nowise enter into it anything that defileth, neither whatsoever worketh abomination, or maketh a lie: but they which are written in the Lamb's book of life" (Rev. 21:27). All who are there will be one in faith and in knowledge. They are there, not because of their works, lest they should boast, but because they have washed their robes and made them white in the blood of the Lamb (Rev. 7:14). They are clean in pure surroundings.

To go through death's door means to join the collective citizenry of the Kingdom of God that lies beyond. "But ye are come unto Mount Zion, and unto the city of the living God, the heavenly Jerusalem, and to an innumerable company of angels to the general assembly and church of the first-born, which are written in heaven, and to God the judge of all, and to the spirits of just men made perfect" (Heb. 12:22, 23).

Christian death is therefore less to be feared than to be welcomed. While it takes us from persons and things held dear, it makes possible the full enjoyment of the "unsearchable riches of Christ" which are now known and experienced only faintly and imperfectly.

What Do We Know of the Life After Death?

"The dust returns to the earth as it was, and the spirit returns unto God who gave it" (Eccles. 12:7). Our new spiritual body shall be "fashioned like unto his glorious body" (Phil. 3:21), the resurrection-body of Jesus. This new body will be our means of self-manifestation and intercommunion. Over against a long unconscious sleep, we are assured that *"Today thou shalt be with me in Paradise"* (Luke 23:43). In the parable of the rich man and Lazarus as well as in the transfiguration scene, Old and New Testament persons recognize each other.

While the words of Jesus about marriage have been thought to weaken the gospel of reunion with and recognition of loved ones ("In heaven they neither marry nor are given in marriage, but are as the angels of God," Matt. 22:30), these words do not mean that husband or wife will not be uniquely related to each other in spiritual fellowship, that family relationships will lose all meaning. They do mean that the reproduction of the race will cease. It is quite conceivable that uncongenial bonds, perhaps largely physical on this side, and thus unhappy, will not hold two natures together on the other side, but Jesus never said a word against the continuance of that exalted fellowship of spirit with spirit which real lovers hold dearest in marriage. In fact, this very passaage, by emphasizing "I am the God of Abraham, of Isaac and of Jacob. God is not the God of the dead but of the living," is one of the clearest and most forceful statements for the continuance of personal existence, which, of course, cannot be unrelated to the experiences that have caused that person to be what he is, or has become.

> To be in heaven as Christianity conceives it, is to be a member of a society of persons who seek God, themselves, and each other as all truly are, without confusion or illusion, and love God, themselves and each other with the love of this true insight.
> — TAYLOR, *Christian Hope of Immortality*, pp. 80-81

Add to this Jesus' words, "I will come again and receive you unto myself; that where I am there ye may be also" (John 14:3), and "Father, I desire that they also, whom thou hast given me, be with me where I am: that they may behold my glory, which thou hast given me: for thou lovedst me before the foundation of the world" (John 17:24); and then we may say, "Heaven is where Jesus is," and that may well suffice for us.

Jesus speaks repeatedly of heaven as the dwelling place of God and the destination of His children: "Our Father who art in heaven" (Matt. 6:19, 20). "Lay not up for yourselves treasures upon earth, where moth and rust doth corrupt, and where thieves break through and steal: but lay up for yourselves treasures in heaven, where neither moth nor rust doth corrupt, and where thieves do not break through nor steal: For where your treasure is, there will your heart be also" (Matt. 6: 19, 21). The writer to the Hebrews mentions "a better country, that is, an heavenly" (11:12), "the heavenly Jerusalem" (12:22).

Shall We Know Each Other There?

No question concerning the future is asked more frequently nor more earnestly. Heaven would lose much of its attractiveness, say many, if that privilege is not to be expected. Some go so far as to say they would rather not live if they are to live forever without renewing the fellowship of loved ones who have gone before.

It is helpful to remember that this is a universal hope

which dates back as far as human history extends. Plato recognized and spoke of it freely. Virgil recorded it. The Hindu incorporated it in his creed. The Egyptians embalmed their dead in the hope of it. The universality of it, the fact that God endowed man with such a universal hope, would seem to be a strong presumption, if not proof, in favor of the belief that Christians will know one another in the future life.

But the Scriptures again offer us far more than hope; they bring conviction and clarity. The believer is promised not less but more knowledge in the eternal home. "Now we see through a glass darkly, but then face to face; now I know in part, but then shall I know even as also I am known" (I Cor. 13:12). Is it not logical to infer that with this increased knowledge, there will come a better acquaintance with others than ever before?

"Rejoice not," said Jesus, "that the devils are subject to you, but rather rejoice because your names are written in heaven" (Luke 10:20). "I am the God of Abraham, and the God of Isaac and the God of Jacob. God is not the God of the dead but of the living" (Matt. 22:32). Abraham is still Abraham; Isaac still Isaac, — identifiable, self-conscious personalities. In the parable of The Rich Man and Lazarus, recognition is either stated or assumed. So also in the transfiguration scene we see a Peter, James, John, Moses and Elias — all as individuals who have retained their personal identity. But most illuminating of all is the record concerning Jesus and his disciples during the forty days. Jesus was changed and glorified yet, recognizable and identifiable by the Eleven.

Above all, let us not forget that Jesus is the center of salvation and of the heavenly life. It is He who makes loved ones the more precious, and fellowship truly satisfying even here and now. How much more so, yonder: "Where I am there shall my servant be also; That where I am there ye may be also. Father, I will that they also whom thou hast given me be with *me.*" He is evidently counting on being with His own; and His own should be counting on being with Him and with those who are His.

How Are the Dead Raised
And With What Manner of Body Do They Come?
(I Cor. 15:35)

Paul gives us the answer very specifically. "You foolish man. What you sow does not come to life unless it dies. And what you sow is not the body which is to be, but a bare kernel, perhaps of wheat or of some other grain. But God gives it a body as he has chosen, and to each kind of seed its own body. For not all flesh is alike but there is one kind for men, another for animals, another for birds, and another for fish. There are celestial bodies and there are terrestrial bodies; but the glory of the celestial is one, and the glory of the terrestrial is another. There is one glory of the sun, and another glory of the moon, and another glory of the stars; for star differs from star in glory.

"So it is with the resurrection of the dead. What is

sown is perishable, what is raised is imperishable. It is sown in dishonor, it is raised in glory. It is sown in weakness, it is raised in power. It is sown a physical body, it is raised a spiritual body. If there is a physical body, there is also a spiritual body. Thus it is written, The first man Adam became a living being; the last Adam became a life-giving spirit. But it is not the spiritual which is first but the physical, and then the spiritual. The first man was from the earth, a man of dust, so are those who are of the dust; and as is the man of heaven, so are those who are of heaven. Just as we have borne the image of the man of dust, we shall also bear the image of the man of heaven. I tell you this, brethren: flesh and blood cannot inherit the kingdom of God, nor does the perishable inherit the imperishable.

"Lo! I tell you a mystery. We shall not all sleep, but we shall all be changed, in a moment, in the twinkling of an eye, at the last trumpet. For the trumpet will sound, and the dead will be raised imperishable, and we shall be changed. For this perishable nature must put on the imperishable, and this mortal nature must put on immortality. When the perishable puts on the imperishable, and the mortal puts on immortality, then shall come to pass the saying that is written: 'Death is swallowed up in victory'" (I Cor. 15:36-54, RSV).

If we note carefully Jesus' post-resurrection body as it appears during the forty days and remember that "our conversation [citizenship] is in heaven," then I

Cor. 15:44 takes on real meaning, "It is sown a natural body, it is raised a spiritual body. There is a natural body, and there is a spiritual body." Similarly, II Cor. 5:1-4: "For we know that if our earthly house of this tabernacle were dissolved, we have a building of God, an house not made with hands, eternal in the heavens. For in this we groan, earnestly desiring to be clothed upon with our house which is from heaven if so be that being clothed we shall not be found naked. For we that are in this tabernacle do groan, being burdened: not for that we would be unclothed, but clothed upon, that mortality might be swallowed up of life."

This says, primarily, that we are to be, not disembodied spirits; not ghosts, but redeemed human beings; for Christianity is concerned with the redemption of the body as well as the soul.

Dr. Charles Hodge, in his theology, has suggested that; ". . . they probably err who suppose that heaven is too radically different from life and society here. Perhaps if they could imagine a state of human society from which all evil and all that belongs to a temporal and fleshly condition are eliminated, they could get a fair mental picture of the realm of the redeemed. But the trouble is that the imagination is hardly equal to that task. People are so tied to the sinful and the fleshly and the temporal that the imagination staggers in the effort to picture a state without these things."

When Paul looked to the realm beyond death, he did not think of it in terms of his bodily life which is marked by *corruption, dishonor* and *weakness*. Rather did he look for a body of *incorruption, glory* and *strength*. Instead of a natural body he assures us we shall have a spiritual body. As God provides bodies terrestrial and celestial, so will he provide an appropriate organ, a glorified body, for our spirit. It is sufficient, then, to know, "God giveth it a body as it pleased him" (I Cor. 15:38). It is no more wonderful that we shall live again than that we live now; it is no more wonderful that we shall be human beings and have a body then than that we have a body now. Surely it is enough to satisfy anyone to know that his body will be like Christ's glorified, post-resurrection body throughout eternity!

Can We Commune With The Departed?

In the Apostles' Creed we confess, "I believe in the communion of saints." Too often that means to us merely the fellowship of those who gather with us around the Lord's table. The words found in the communion forms or liturgies of many churches seem to suggest a much wider fellowship: "Thee, mighty God, heavenly King, we magnify and praise. With patriarchs and prophets, apostles and martyrs; with the Holy Church throughout all the world; with the Heavenly Jerusalem, the joyful assembly and congregation of the first born on high; with the innumerable company of angels round about thy throne, the heaven of heavens, and all the powers therein; we worship and adore thy glorious Name, saying Holy, holy, holy, Lord God of

Hosts, heaven and earth are full of thy glory; Glory be to thee, O Lord most high.

"We give thanks unto thee for thy grace and gifts bestowed on those who have thus gone before us in the way of salvation and by whom we are now compassed about in our Christian course, as a cloud of witnesses looking down upon us from the heavenly world. Enable us to follow their faith, that we may enter at death into their joy; and so abide with them in rest and peace till both they and we shall reach our common consummation of redemption and bliss in the glorious resurrection of the last day."

Certainly this article of our faith refers to those still "in the body," but does it not also include those "passed through the body and gone?"

To communicate means "to give by way of information"; to commune means "to hold spiritual intercourse." While Spiritualism demands communication, the Christian is content with communion, a fellowship of spirit with spirit. Communion is higher, closer, more intimate than communication and the highest communion of all is one without words, because it is above words.

> I watch thee from the quiet shore
> Thy spirit up to mine can reach,
> But in dear words of human speech
> We two communicate no more.
>
> — TENNYSON,
> *In Memoriam, LXXXV*

At first thought we might speak of the cruel hand of death here but that is only a part of the total picture. We would like to see each person grow up to maturity, enjoy a comfortable pleasant life's evening and then fall asleep. But this world does not operate thus. The consequences of sin, man's willfulness and waywardness alone, not to mention disease, accidents and catastrophes, cause quite a different result.

Recognizing life as it is, what can we say to the question above? When Jesus was hanging on the cross, He gave us the answer: "Woman, behold thy son; Son, Behold thy mother." Commit your loved ones to the care of trusted relatives and friends; above all, to Him who is a Father whose gracious Providence carried you through the crises of your life and led you on paths you could not have imagined possible in earlier years.

V

ETERNAL

LIFE NOW!

Eternal life is not life *after death* but it is the kind of life that is *above* death. "He that believeth on the Son, *has* eternal life" (John 3:36). Eternal life begins here and now. Not death but *regeneration,* the new birth, is the portal through which we enter upon it.

"Verily, verily, I say unto you, He that heareth my word, and believeth on him that sent me, hath everlasting life, and shall not come into condemnation; but is passed from death unto life.

Verily, verily, I say unto you, The hour is coming, and now is, when the dead shall hear the voice of the Son of God: and they that hear shall live" (John 5: 24, 25).

The same experience is referred to in the remarkable

inheritance which Peter describes, "Blessed be the God and Father of our Lord Jesus Christ, which according to his abundant mercy hath begotten us again unto a lively hope by the resurrection of Jesus Christ from the dead, to an inheritance incorruptible, and undefiled, and that fadeth not away, reserved in heaven for you, who are kept by the power of God through faith unto salvation ready to be revealed in the last time" (I Peter 1:3-5). Over against decay and corruption, this is incorruptible; over against the imperfections and impurities so common here, this is undefiled. While earthly possessions and glories lose their value and luster, this inheritance does not fade.

Inheritance implies something not earned, an unmerited gift. "The wages of sin is death, but the gift of God is eternal life through Jesus Christ our Lord" (Rom. 6:23).

"Being justified by faith, we have peace with God through our Lord Jesus Christ" (Rom. 5:1). "There is now, therefore, no condemnation to them which are in Christ Jesus, who walk not after the flesh, but after the Spirit. For the law of the Spirit of life in Christ Jesus hath made me free from the law of sin and death" (Rom. 8:1, 2).

This faith, this hope becomes an incentive to thankful holy living in the present. The apostle Peter urges believers to purity of life by saying that, since the believer is looking "for new heavens and a new earth, wherein dwelleth righteousness," he should be diligent that he "may be found of him in peace, without spot, and blameless" (II Pet. 3:11-14). Every honest student of the Word of God has recognized this principle of basing the appeal to holy living on the character of the life to come, and has felt its incentive to holiness of life. One cannot be worldly in life, impure in heart, unrighteous in business, slothful in the Lord's work if he really desires to share in the glory of the life to come. "And every one that hath this hope in him purifieth himself, even as he is pure" (I John 3:3).

Again, this faith impels "growing in the grace and knowledge of our Lord and Saviour Jesus Christ (II Peter 3:18). In writing to the Corinthians, Paul declares, "But we all, with open (unveiled) face beholding as in a glass the glory of the Lord, are changed into the same image from glory to glory, even as by the Spirit of the Lord" (II Cor. 3:18). There is the idea of a growing likeness between the believer and the Saviour as he continues to gaze upon Him with the eye of faith.

For those who have entered upon eternal life here, death is but a passing incident, for it leads to a continuation of that life that has been begun here.

Percy Ainsworth expresses it pointedly in his poem, "And the Life Everlasting:"

It is not something yet to be revealed —
  The everlasting life — 'tis here and now;
Passing unseen because our eyes are sealed
  With blindness for the pride upon our brow.

It dwells not in innumerable years;
  It is the breath of God in timeless things —

The strong, divine persistence that inheres
   In Love's red pulses and in Faith's white wings.

It is the power whereby low lives aspire
   Unto the doing of a selfless deed,
Unto the slaying of a soft desire,
   In the service of a high, unwordly creed.

And if we feel it not amid our strife,
   In all our toiling and in all our pain —
This rhythmic pulsing of eternal life —
   Then do we work and suffer here in vain.

VI

REMEMBERING THEM

WITHOUT PAIN

We have been directed to the source of comfort, courage and strength that is more than able to sustain us when loved ones are called home.

"Blessed be God, even the Father of our Lord Jesus Christ, the Father of mercies, and the God of all comfort; Who comforteth us in all our tribulation, that we may be able to comfort them which are in any trouble, by the comfort wherewith we ourselves are comforted of God" (II Cor. 1:3, 4).

Pain of parting there will be for a time. That is inevitable since we are constituted as we are and find ourselves in the kind of world that we dwell in; but the Lord "sendeth forth His word and healeth us. He

healeth the broken in heart" (Ps. 107:20); "his healing
shall spring forth speedily" (Isa. 58:8).

"Your grief is but the measure of your love." But it
is not necessary that the adjustments required will be
complex and require a long period of time. More
significant than time and details of adjustment is the
quality and depth of the Christian faith which is ours.

Love and fear are inseparable. The heart which
loves is the heart which aches and its suffering will be
proportionate to its tenderness.

Loss and Fear

Were loss not always to be feared;
Were every joy we gain secure;
From hazards were all roadways cleared
And every plan and purpose sure;
Were hearts and minds from worry freed,
For love there would be little need.

But love and fear walk side by side,
Since all we cherish most is frail;
By heartache often love is tried.
Love worries lest its care may fail
Love strives to hold at any cost
The precious joys that may be lost.

— Edgar A. Guest

The antidote for such fear of loss is not a fleeing
from love, a hardening of one's heart, but the recognition that with *faith* and *hope*, *love* constitutes the
"everlasting trio" and is even the greatest of the three
(I Cor. 13). It is the binding force that unites persons

68

in most blessed and satisfying relationships to one another and to God.

So we would not counteract love by cauterizing the wound of bereavement through forgetfulness, nor by dulling its pain by a calloused insensibility. That would be substituting an anesthetic for a remedy. The death of loved ones could be robbed of its terrors by rooting them out of our lives but it would mean destroying the most meaningful and cherished values that unite us to others and the best that is in ourselves.

Knowing that our loved ones live on, have been merely called home, we aim not at insensibility nor disloyal forgetfulness. Rather do we cherish their memory and recognize that being "at home with the Lord" is far better.

Love Can Never Lose Its Own

Yet love will dream, and faith will trust
  (Since He who knows our need is just),
That somehow, somewhere, meet we must.
  Alas for him who never sees
The stars shine through his cypress-trees!
  Who, hopeless, lays his dead away,
Nor looks to see the breaking day
  Across the mournful marbles play!
Who hath not learned, in hours of faith,
  The truth to flesh and sense unknown,
That life is ever lord of death,
  And love can never lose its own!

                           — John G. Whittier

With God

More homelike seems the vast unknown
　Since loved ones entered there;
To follow them were not so hard,
　Wherever they may fare.
They cannot be where God is not,
　On any sea or shore;
Whate'er betides, Thy love abides,
　Our God, forevermore.
　　　　　　　　　— John W. Chadwick

For the present then, while the wound is in the process of healing, we sing —

Let sorrow do its work,
Send grief and pain;
Sweet are thy messengers,
Sweet their refrain.
When they can sing with me
More love, O Christ to Thee.
More love to Thee,
More love to Thee!

Thus the same faith that comforts us when loved ones are called home, will serve at the same time to prepare us for our own home-going whenever our Lord calls.

Then shall my latest breath
Whisper thy praise;
This be the parting cry
My heart shall raise;
This still its prayer shall be,
More love, O Christ, to Thee
More love to Thee,
More love to Thee!

70